CODE BREAKERS AND SPIES

Code Breakers and Spies of
World War I

JEANNE MARIE FORD

Cavendish
Square
New York

Published in 2019 by Cavendish Square Publishing, LLC
243 5th Avenue, Suite 136, New York, NY 10016

Library of Congress Cataloging-in-Publication Data

Names: Ford, Jeanne Marie, 1971- author.
Title: Code breakers and spies of World War I / Jeanne Marie Ford.
Description: New York : Cavendish Square, 2019. | Series: Code breakers and
spies | Includes bibliographical references and index. | Audience: Grades 7-12.
Identifiers: LCCN 2017052584 (print) | LCCN 2017053481 (ebook) |
ISBN 9781502638502 (library bound) |
ISBN 9781502638519 (pbk.) | ISBN 9781502638526 (ebook)
Subjects: LCSH: World War, 1914-1918--Secret service--Juvenile literature. |
World War, 1914-1918--Military intelligence--Juvenile literature. | Spies--
History--20th century--Juvenile literature. | Cryptography--History--20th
century--Juvenile literature. | Espionage--History--20th century--Juvenile
literature. | Military intelligence--History--20th century--Juvenile literature.
Classification: LCC D639.S7 (ebook) | LCC D639.
S7 F67 2019 (print) | DDC 940.4/85--dc23
LC record available at https://lccn.loc.gov/2017052584

Editorial Director: David McNamara
Editor: Stacy Orlando
Copy Editor: Alex Tessman
Associate Art Director: Amy Greenan
Designer: Joe Parenteau
Production Coordinator: Karol Szymczuk
Photo Research: J8 Media

The photographs in this book are used by permission and through the courtesy of: Cover, p. 1 Doug Steley B/
Alamy Stock Photo; p. 4 William L. Clements Library, University of Michigan; p. 9 Library of Congress;
p. 12 Library of Congress/Wikimedia Commons/File:First_flight2.jpg/CC PD; p. 18 Historicair/Wikimedia
Commons/File:Beale 3.svg/CC BY-SA 3.0; p. 20 Archive PL/Alamy Stock Photo; p. 25 ChickiBam/
iStock; p. 29 Paul J. Richards/AFP/Getty Images; p. 31 Bettmann/Getty Images; p. 34 US Signal Corps/
The LIFE Picture Collection/Getty Images; p. 38 De Agostini Picture Library/Getty Images; p. 40 National
Archives and Records Administration/Wikimedia Commons/File:Zimmermann Telegram as Received by
the German Ambassador to Mexico – NARA – 302025.jpg/CC PD; p. 42 2nd Lt. D McLellan/Imperial
War Museums/Getty Images; p. 45 Fine Art Images/Heritage Images/Hulton Archive/Getty Images;
p. 47 Herbert O. Yardley/Wikimedia Commons/File:Victoria scarf.png/CC PD; p. 54 Central Intelligence
Agency/Wikimedia Commons/File:Enigma-Machine.jpg/CC PD; p. 58 Rodger Mallison/Fort Worth
Star-Telegram/MCT/Tribune News Service/Getty Images; p. 61 Hubert Berberich/Wikimedia Commons/
File:CipherDisk2000.jpg/CC PD; p. 63 Greg Hume/Wikimedia Commons/File:KetteringAerialTorpedo.
jpg/CC BY-SA 3.0; p. 69 Hulton Archive/Getty Images; p. 71 Saul Loeb/AFP/Getty Images.

Printed in the United States of America

Contents

Dr Sir

Sir W. Howe
is gone to the
Chesapeak bay with
the greatest part of the
army. I hear he is
landed but am not
certain I am
left to command
here with
too small a force
to make any effectual
diversion in your favour
I shall try something
at any rate. It may be of use
to you. I own to you I think
Sr Wm's move just at this time
the worst he could take
much joy on your suc

THE HISTORY OF INTELLIGENCE

Spies have lived among us for thousands of years, and the same basic methods were used until the beginning of the twentieth century. Messages and maps were written by hand. Invisible ink or codes disguised information. Papers were hidden in secret compartments and carried on foot or horseback into enemy territory. Eavesdropping involved listening in person from a nearby location. These early practices became the foundation for spy craft, or the art of spying, which has grown increasingly sophisticated over time.

OPPOSITE:
Hidden messages in certain letters are revealed through the use of a unique template, or "mask."

The Birth of American Intelligence

During the American Revolution, George Washington headed a large network of soldiers, as well as a group of civilians known as the Culper Spy Ring. Washington knew his army had less training and manpower than the British did. The Americans would need to outsmart the enemy in order to win, and Washington became a spymaster.

Washington worked with a chemist, the brother of future Supreme Court Chief Justice John Jay, to develop better secret inks. He used a variety of creative means to transmit secret information. For example, a black petticoat hung on a clothesline meant that documents should be retrieved from a secret dead drop location. His spies used code names, ciphers, and disinformation to trick the enemy. A defeated British officer said that Washington did not outfight the enemy; rather, he out-spied them.

Brother Against Brother

During the American Civil War, the proximity of the two enemies and lack of a physical border made spies central to the conflict. Elizabeth Van Lew was a Southern resident but a Northern sympathizer and abolitionist. She managed to build a substantial spy ring known as the Richmond Underground that included slaves, one of whom, Mary Bowser, served as a waitress in the Confederacy's White House. Bowser could listen in on the conversations of Confederate President Jefferson Davis and report them back to Van Lew. Van Lew also sent African American couriers with coded messages hidden inside fake eggs or servants' dresses.

Female spies often sent important intelligence across enemy lines inside bandages or knitting yarn. Confederate spy Rose O'Neal Greenhow pinned coded messages into the hair of her courier, Betty Duval. When the head of the US Secret Service put Greenhow under house arrest, she still did not give up her espionage activities. She would rearrange her

DID YOU KNOW?

The Bible depicts one of the earliest recorded examples of intelligence gathering. When the Israelites approached the Promised Land, God ordered Moses to send men ahead of him to get the lay of the land. Today, such a mission would be called reconnaissance.

house shutters or use certain colors in her embroidery to convey specific messages.

Spies would continue to use couriers who carried information in ever-more-clever ways; however, technology at the dawn of the twentieth century would forever change the methods by which information was gathered and shared both for military and civilian use.

New Technology

The nineteenth century was a period of great innovation and discovery. The United States entered what is known as the Gilded Age as both population and industry grew. With the spread of electricity, many powered technologies were invented, which impacted military and civilian communications.

Telegraph to Telephone

In 1844, Samuel Morse sent the first electric telegraph message in America. Morse code, a combination of dots and dashes representing each letter of the alphabet, allowed messages to be conveyed by electronic pulses across many miles. Thousands of miles of telegraph cables laid across the Atlantic Ocean sent messages around the globe. Information that had taken weeks to transmit could suddenly be received almost instantly.

The US Military Telegraph Corps played an integral role in intelligence work for the Union in the Civil War and operated from 1861 until 1866.

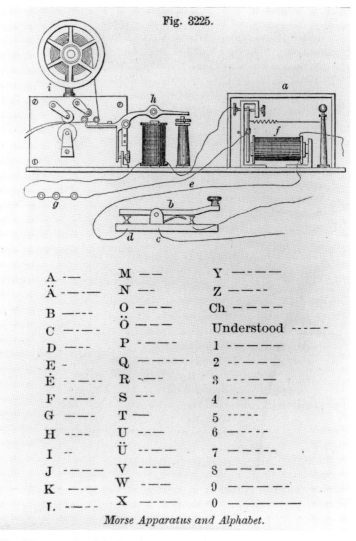

The Morse code alphabet is a series of dots and dashes originally used for sending telegrams.

During major battles, President Lincoln would sleep in the telegraph office of the War Department so that he could receive up-to-the-minute reports from the field. He used this information to formulate the orders he then transmitted to generals via telegraph.

Telegrams were used as a means for communication for more than 150 years. The telephone, invented by Alexander Graham Bell in 1876, would eventually replace the telegraph. Western Union, which has offered telegraph service since 1861, sent as many as sixty million telegrams per year during its peak.

Telegraph and telephone signals traveled across wires from one fixed point to another. Therefore, they were useless on ships and any area that was not serviced by an existing cable. Naval vessels communicated by waving semaphore flags in patterns of movement that stood for letters of the alphabet. Semaphore signaling was a time-consuming process that worked only when senders and receivers were within visual contact of one another.

On Radio Waves

Guglielmo Marconi's invention of the radio in 1897 would have a radical effect on communication across the globe. Wireless radio allowed voice signals to travel through the air. Radio would change everyday life in terms of access to news and entertainment. Its value was immediately evident to sailors. Had more ships been equipped with radios when the *Titanic* sank in 1912, its distress SOS would have been heard by several other nearby vessels. Many more lives could have been saved.

Radio would forever change the way wars were fought as information could travel to ships, planes, and other places that could not be reliably reached by telegraph wires. Yet radio messages were broadcast publicly and broadcasted information could be easily intercepted, making cryptography and military intelligence increasingly important tools of warfare at the outset of the twentieth century.

Through the Skies

As Marconi was developing his revolutionary means of communication, a new means of transportation was taking form in America. Brothers Orville and Wilbur Wright successfully piloted the first airplane in 1903.

The airplane was not the first "flying machine." During the United States Civil War, Thaddeus Lowe used hot air balloons for surveillance of battlegrounds and troop movements. He even took a telegraph wire into the air and would send his real-time observations to military headquarters. He tried to take advantage

The Wright brothers piloted the world's first successful airplane flight in 1903.

of another new invention, photography, to capture details of the landscape and enemy troops.

The Germans developed zeppelins, or blimps, that could transport more people across greater distances than hot air balloons. These were even more useful for spying because they could be steered with much more precision. Airplanes were yet another step forward. Planes would change the way wars were fought, as they could be outfitted to drop bombs from the sky. Airplanes would also provide a huge advance in the art of aerial surveillance.

Automobiles were invented at the turn of the twentieth century, and Thomas Edison developed the first working light bulb in 1879. As information and people traveled faster, new ideas also spread more rapidly.

World Revolutions

Over fifty countries experienced political upheaval in 1848, as peasants across Europe rose up against the oppression of kings and tyrants. In Prussia, a police officer named Wilhelm Stieber helped save King Frederick William IV from an angry mob during the 1848 revolution. Some believe that Stieber himself paid the rioters so that he could play the role of hero. The rebels lost the war, and the king held on to his power. He rewarded Stieber with the job of Chief of Police.

The Prince of Spies

The ruthless Stieber gradually built a huge network of up to 35,000 informants throughout Europe. He compiled massive intelligence reports for the Prussian army, which went on to have a succession of military victories over the next decade. After most of the German states were united under Prussian rule, the Prussians set their sights on the Austrian Empire.

Stieber disguised himself as a peddler and went out into the streets of Austria to obtain information firsthand. He provided the army with detailed intelligence about the Austrians, which helped achieve a decisive victory. Next, the Prussians turned toward France. Stieber traveled the French countryside. He sent women into homes disguised as maids to spy on officials. He sent farm workers into the fields to "help" farmers harvest their crops. He ultimately compiled over one thousand reports about the French landscape, including minute details such as the locations of individual horses. With this cache of information in hand, Prussia captured Paris in 1871.

Stieber was a successful man but not an honorable one. He used the intelligence he gathered to blackmail many rich and famous Germans. Huge crowds attended his funeral in 1882, many of them overjoyed that he was finally dead.

Known as the Prince of Spies, Stieber is considered one of the fathers of modern intelligence gathering. He used his web of spies to control the German press and the banking system. He helped invent psychological warfare (psyops), which involves manipulating people's minds. One technique he used was to widely publicize bad news about the enemy to raise the morale of his own people. The unrest and distrust his tactics stoked would help set the stage for World War I.

Spy Fever

Spy fever soon ran rampant in Europe. Germany's conquering march across Europe left many in Great

Britain fearful that their nation might soon be invaded. Popular English novels in the early 1900s depicted nefarious German spies. Many British citizens believed their society had been infiltrated by a ring of undercover agents. As the public's fears grew, the British government began to develop a plan to fight espionage. The Secret Service Bureau was the result. Formed in 1909, it later became the Directorate of Military Intelligence Section 5, or MI5. It groomed several successful agents during this time, including Sidney Reilly, whose exploits later inspired a television miniseries and Ian Fleming's James Bond.

The leader of the Secret Service Bureau, Vernon Kell, eventually identified twenty-two German plants operating in the country. As tensions between nations grew, Kell successfully removed twenty-one of the infiltrators from the field. British spy fears turned out to have been wildly overblown. However, the mass hysteria led to the creation of MI5, which would prove crucial in the years to follow.

Codes and Ciphers

Information transmitted by spies is often kept secure by encoding it. Codes and ciphers are the two major methods of encrypting intelligence. A code is used in conjunction with a codebook. Each code word listed in the book is substituted for a word or phrase from the original text. A cipher either substitutes or rearranges individual letters of the plaintext based on an algorithm.

Julius Caesar introduced the first modern intelligence system. A former soldier, he knew that accurate information about the enemy was vital to winning battles. He and his successor, Caesar Augustus, developed a network of spies that fanned out across the entire Roman Empire. Julius Caesar is also credited with developing a well-known cipher for sending coded messages, known today as the Caesar Cipher. If his correspondence was intercepted, the enemy would not know what it said.

The Caesar Cipher involved simple substitution and became too easy to crack as communication methods grew more sophisticated.. A more complex substitution, the Vignère Cipher, was developed in the sixteenth century. It was considered unbreakable for nearly three centuries. Charles Babbage is likely the first person to figure out how to reliably crack the code, sometime around 1854.

Public interest in codes and ciphers increased around the same time. The invention of the telegraph was partly responsible. Telegrams had to be fairly short

John Wilkie and the Spanish Spy Ring

America entered the Spanish-American War in 1898 after a US Naval ship was sunk off the coast of Cuba. While the war was primarily fought in Cuba and the Philippines, the Spaniards launched an information war from Montreal, Canada.

In an effort to uncover the Spanish spy ring, US Secret Service Chief John Wilkie sent two agents to break into the Montreal home of the Spanish ambassador, Ramon de Carranza, while he was out having breakfast one day. They took a letter from his desk that implicated him as a spy and published it in a newspaper. Carranza claimed that the letter had been forged. An unpleasant diplomatic incident followed, and the ambassador was forced to return to Spain under a cloud of international suspicion.

After the United States won the war, a Canadian man named George Bell came forward. Bell claimed he had stolen a letter, but that Wilkie had ordered a forgery published in the newspaper. Another Secret Service agent disputed Bell's version of events, stating he was the one responsible for the theft of the letter and that there had been no forgery.

The truth remains murky to this day. However, there is no question that Wilkie's methods were a sign that increasingly complex subterfuge would become the norm among spies in the new century.

317, 8, 92, 73, 112, 89, 67, 318, 28, 96, 107, 41, 631, 78, 146, 397, 118, 98, 114,
246, 348, 116, 74, 88, 12, 65, 32, 14, 81, 19, 76, 121, 216, 85, 33, 66, 15, 108, 68,
77, 43, 24, 122, 96, 117, 36, 211, 301, 15, 44, 11, 46, 89, 18, 136, 68, 317, 28, 90,
82, 304, 71, 43, 221, 198, 176, 310, 319, 81, 99, 264, 380, 56, 37, 319, 2, 44, 53,
28, 44, 75, 98, 102, 37, 85, 107, 117, 64, 88, 136, 48, 154, 99, 175, 89, 315, 326,
78, 96, 214, 218, 311, 43, 89, 51, 90, 75, 128, 96, 33, 28, 103, 84, 65, 26, 41, 246,
84, 270, 98, 116, 32, 59, 74, 66, 69, 240, 15, 8, 121, 20, 77, 89, 31, 11, 106, 81,
191, 224, 328, 18, 75, 52, 82, 117, 201, 39, 23, 217, 27, 21, 84, 35, 54, 109, 128,
49, 77, 88, 1, 81, 217, 64, 55, 83, 116, 251, 269, 311, 96, 54, 32, 120, 18, 132, 102,
219, 211, 84, 150, 219, 275, 312, 64, 10, 106, 87, 75, 47, 21, 29, 37, 81, 44, 18,
126, 115, 132, 160, 181, 203, 76, 81, 299, 314, 337, 351, 96, 11, 28, 97, 318, 238,
106, 24, 93, 3, 19, 17, 26, 60, 73, 88, 14, 126, 138, 234, 286, 297, 321, 365, 264,
19, 22, 84, 56, 107, 98, 123, 111, 214, 136, 7, 33, 45, 40, 13, 28, 46, 42, 107, 196,
227, 344, 198, 203, 247, 116, 19, 8, 212, 230, 31, 6, 328, 65, 48, 52, 59, 41, 122,
33, 117, 11, 18, 25, 71, 36, 45, 83, 76, 89, 92, 31, 65, 70, 83, 96, 27, 33, 44, 50, 61,
24, 112, 136, 149, 176, 180, 194, 143, 171, 205, 296, 87, 12, 44, 51, 89, 98, 34, 41,
208, 173, 66, 9, 35, 16, 95, 8, 113, 175, 90, 56, 203, 19, 177, 183, 206, 157, 200,
218, 260, 291, 305, 618, 951, 320, 18, 124, 78, 65, 19, 32, 124, 48, 53, 57, 84, 96,
207, 244, 66, 82, 119, 71, 11, 86, 77, 213, 54, 82, 316, 245, 303, 86, 97, 106, 212,
18, 37, 15, 81, 89, 16, 7, 81, 39, 96, 14, 43, 216, 118, 29, 55, 109, 136, 172, 213,
64, 8, 227, 304, 611, 221, 364, 819, 375, 128, 296, 1, 18, 53, 76, 10, 15, 23, 19, 71,
84, 120, 134, 66, 73, 89, 96, 230, 48, 77, 26, 101, 127, 936, 218, 439, 178, 171, 61,
226, 313, 215, 102, 18, 167, 262, 114, 218, 66, 59, 48, 27, 19, 13, 82, 48, 162, 119,
34, 127, 139, 34, 128, 129, 74, 63, 120, 11, 54, 61, 73, 92, 180, 66, 75, 101, 124,
265, 89, 96, 126, 274, 896, 917, 434, 461, 235, 890, 312, 413, 328, 381, 96, 105,
217, 66, 118, 22, 77, 64, 42, 12, 7, 55, 24, 83, 67, 97, 109, 121, 135, 181, 203, 219,
228, 256, 21, 34, 77, 319, 374, 382, 675, 684, 717, 864, 203, 4, 18, 92, 16, 63, 82,
22, 46, 55, 69, 74, 112, 134, 186, 175, 119, 213, 416, 312, 343, 264, 119, 186, 218,
343, 417, 845, 951, 124, 209, 49, 617, 856, 924, 936, 72, 19, 28, 11, 35, 42, 40, 66,
85, 94, 112, 65, 82, 115, 119, 236, 244, 186, 172, 112, 85, 6, 56, 38, 44, 85, 72,
32, 47, 73, 96, 124, 217, 314, 319, 221, 644, 817, 821, 934, 922, 416, 975, 10, 22,
18, 46, 137, 181, 101, 39, 86, 103, 116, 138, 164, 212, 218, 296, 815, 380, 412,
460, 495, 675, 820, 952.

The ciphers contained in the 1885 Beale Papers have also been
used to train American code breakers.

due to the constraints of Morse Code. Telegraph operators could send longer and more complex messages with the help of a codebook that mapped whole sentences to single words. They also had to read every message they sent. If a message was very personal in nature, its sender might want to encrypt it.

Privacy likewise motivated young Victorians, who lived by a strict code of conduct. Afraid their parents might intercept their love letters, couples resorted to sending coded messages to each other through the newspaper's personal columns. This trend led to the appearance of cryptology puzzles in the newspaper. Writers such as Jules Verne, Sir Arthur Conan Doyle, and Edgar Allan Poe also included ciphers in their popular works.

In 1885 a mysterious pamphlet circulated in America, advertising a treasure that had allegedly been buried years before in Virginia. The location of the treasure was supposed to be revealed through a long numerical cipher contained in the three-part text, called the Beale ciphers. Future cryptanalysts Herbert O. Yardley and Colonel William Friedman became very interested in the Beale ciphers. Friedman eventually made them a part of the training program for new code breakers. The first and third ciphers, which supposedly contain the location of the treasure, remained unsolved to this day.

THE WORLD AT WAR

In 1914 a single bullet sparked a worldwide conflict that lasted four years. Long-simmering tensions in Europe came to a head when Austria-Hungary's Archduke Franz Ferdinand visited Sarajevo, Bosnia. Serbian nationalists were angry that Austria had taken control of Bosnia. They believed it should belong to Serbia. These nationalists formed a secret group called the Black Hand Society. They thought eliminating Ferdinand would help their cause. His visit presented the perfect opportunity. A member of the Black Hand Society shot Ferdinand in the neck, and he died.

OPPOSITE:
Gavrilo Princip (front) and other members of the Black Hand are remembered as heros of Serbian people.

The leaders of Austria-Hungary had no idea the Black Hand Society existed. They blamed the Serbian government for the assassination and immediately declared war. Russia sided with Serbia. Germany defended Austria. Soon, Russia's allies, France and Great Britain, were drawn into the conflict. The British-led side became known as the Allies. The German-led side was called the Central Powers.

The Dawn of Signals Intelligence

Very early on August 5, 1914, just hours after Great Britain had joined the war, the captain of the British ship *Alert* received a coded telegram. The vessel steamed out of port toward the German coast to carry out its orders. The *Alert* was a cable-laying ship with sailors who were experts at finding and repairing underwater telegraph cables, but on this occasion it was on a mission to destroy. The ship lowered its grappling equipment and dredged up the Germans' telegraph cables one by one. They hacked through them and tossed them back into the sea. This was Britain's very first act of war. In an instant, one of the Germans' main avenues of communication with the rest of the world was gone.

Intercepting individual telegrams could be difficult, but radio airwaves were accessible to the public. Anyone could listen to what was being said. Linguists could then easily translate the messages. The Germans could not communicate freely over the radio waves unless they encrypted their messages. Cryptologists, the warring factions quickly realized, could make or break the war effort.

World War I was the first conflict to involve electronic signals intelligence, or the practice of listening in on the enemy's electronic communications. When messages had been carried by hand, they were difficult to steal. Now, although there was a constant wave of incoming information, there was also a severe lack of people qualified to analyze it. Of the warring countries, only France, Russia, and Austria-Hungary had active cryptanalytic departments at the start of the war.

Room 40

The day after the German cables were cut, British Rear Admiral Henry Oliver recruited his friend and Director of Naval Education, Sir Alfred Ewing, to run a section devoted to deciphering enemy signals. Ewing studied cryptology as a hobby but had no training. Up to one hundred enemy messages per day were flooding in via radio, and Ewing knew he would immediately need help. He turned to fellow teachers and staff from the naval colleges Osborne and Dartmouth. A small and somewhat eccentric group toiled in an office of the Admiralty Ripley building in Whitehall that came to be known as Room 40. Classical literature scholar Dillwyn Knox found that he did his best thinking while soaking in a hot bath. Knox would ultimately become a key member of the group, doing much of his work from a tub in the bathroom of his small office in Room 53.

Meanwhile, the Germans had some intelligence successes. The Central Powers had cracked the Russian codes. The Russians knew this but did not have new codes ready to be deployed. Therefore, they sent most of their communication unencrypted over the radio waves and hoped for the best. The Germans listened in and heard the Russians' detailed battle plans. They crushed the Russians in the Battle of Tannenberg during the first month of the war. This was the first time that intercepted radio intelligence ever affected the outcome of a battle.

At first, the code breakers in Room 40 had no idea how to go about translating the encrypted messages. However, they worked together to educate themselves in the field of cryptanalysis. The group also happened upon an extraordinary run of good luck.

German Naval Codebooks Discovered

In mid-August 1914, an Australian naval officer was able to board the German ship *Hobart* docked near Melbourne. He found the captain trying to conceal a set of documents and confiscated them. The papers included one of the German Navy's many codebooks, one of three that would eventually be in the hands of Ewing and Room 40.

Communication codebooks were used to decipher secret messages.

On August 25, the German ship *Magdeburg* ran aground in Estonia. Russians captured several sailors, including the captain, as they tried to evacuate and destroy the ship. Among the surviving papers was another codebook, which contained a map with the location of the German Navy and a cipher key.

Four days later, a British naval patrol sank four German ships. One of the German captains threw the classified documents in his possession overboard. Though they were locked in a waterproof chest, it seemed that they had been lost forever at the bottom of the sea—until November, when a British fishing boat caught the chest in its nets. Within thirteen weeks, the men in Room 40 had obtained all three of the seized German naval codebooks.

Even with these codebooks in hand, the analysts found they still could not decipher most of the signals they were receiving. Finally, Charles Rotter, a German language expert, had a breakthrough. He realized that the messages had been encoded twice. Armed with this knowledge, he approached the code and looked for the most common sets of letters in German as well as the words most likely to be repeated. He ultimately built a key that he shared with the other Room 40 code breakers. The group proceeded to accumulate a huge amount of information from intercepted messages about German naval operations and battle plans.

William Hall

In March of 1915, a group of German soldiers set out for the Middle East, disguising themselves as a traveling circus. Their mission was to persuade the Persians to join the Central Powers. One of the men was separated from the group and surrounded by a British patrol. He fled, wearing nothing but his pajamas. The bags he left behind eventually found their way to Room 40.

At this time, Room 40 and the Intelligence Division had a new director named William Hall, nicknamed 'Blinker' because of a tic that caused him to blink his eyes nervously. Hall ordered the bags to be searched. Folded inside the German's wool underwear was a codebook. In addition to the naval codes, now the Allies had access to the diplomats' codes for sending messages throughout Europe.

Hall began recruiting more analysts who could be taught to crack codes in a highly collaborative environment. Linguists and mathematicians proved particularly valuable. Hall also broke with long-standing tradition and began to hire women with this expertise.

Information from the Skies

Aviators were also breaking new ground during World War I. The first reconnaissance airplane flight set out from France on August 19, 1914, and pilots spotted German troops marching south. The British Army met them on August 22 in their first conflict of the war, the Battle of Mons. The British fought fiercely. What they didn't know was that many German reinforcements were on the way. Pilots conveyed this urgent information to their commander, who ordered his troops to withdraw. While the British were forced to retreat from the battle, this aerial intelligence saved them from a catastrophic defeat.

Despite the new reliance on technology, old-school methods of transmitting information remained important. On the front lines, commanders at the rear needed to be able to receive information from the soldiers in the trenches. Radio and telegrams were not always reliable in the heat of battle as bullets flew.

Homing Pigeons

The British military used more than one hundred thousand homing pigeons to carry messages during the war. The messages had to be short, as they were rolled into metal capsules attached to the birds' legs.

The pigeons lived in mobile lofts near the battlefront and were carried in baskets into the trenches. The birds could quickly deliver information from soldiers on the

Cher Ami, a homing pigeon, saved many lives with the information he carried from the front lines.

front lines to their commanding officers. They could also alert commanders when a soldier was wounded and needed help.

While human couriers presented large moving targets, these trained birds flew so quickly that they were rarely shot down. The war pigeons were successful 95 percent of the time in reaching their intended targets. Commanders considered them so essential to the war effort that in Great Britain, it was illegal to kill or harm one of them. Germans sometimes deployed trained hawks to hunt the enemy's birds on the front lines.

Trained to fly back to their roosts near the commanders, the pigeons would persevere through battle wounds or exhaustion. They served on naval

DID YOU KNOW?

The war's most famous carrier pigeon, Cher Ami, suffered a gunshot wound while carrying information about the location of a lost unit. He lost a leg and an eye but saved the lives of two hundred soldiers. He was awarded a combat medal and was fitted with a wooden leg.

ships and submarines and even in airplanes. The British king sent pigeons from the royal loft to bring him news from the battlefront.

Special Messages

Pigeons were trained to return to their lofts but could not be directed to fly toward a new destination. If a commander wanted to send information to a specific location at the front, he needed a messenger. Soldiers called runners had the most dangerous wartime jobs.

A mixed breed dog named Stubby served with an American unit in seventeen battles.

When it wasn't necessary to deploy a courier who could think on the fly, officers often used dogs to deliver messages instead of people. Because the dogs stood lower to the ground, they were less likely to be hit by gunfire. Soldiers often grew fond of the dogs and were reluctant to send them out in harm's way. Sometimes the soldiers would even choose to run the dog's errands themselves.

Messages sent on the battlefield were often encoded in case they fell into the wrong hands. Soldiers needed codebooks in order to decrypt these messages, which were known as trench codes. Officers had to change the keys often to keep them secure.

The United States intelligence service did not have any trench codes at the beginning of World War I. They barely had an intelligence service. Americans watched warily as war enveloped most of Europe. While many Americans sympathized with the Allies, recent immigrants still had ties to their home countries. Most of the public had a strong desire to remain neutral in the conflict. For two and a half years, Woodrow Wilson managed to keep the United States out of the fray.

ACCOMPLISHMENTS AND BREAKTHROUGHS

A s the war dragged on, the Germans calculated that they could win by disrupting cargo shipments to the Allies. These goods and ammunitions were a lifeline for the Europeans as battles ravaged the continent. Bombs destroyed livestock and crops. While millions of soldiers died in battle, average citizens were dying of starvation.

Curbing these shipments of supplies would involve using submarine warfare to sink vessels in the Atlantic shipping channels. The Germans knew that a policy of deliberately destroying American

OPPOSITE:
The Black Tom Island explosion in 1916 was the result of sabotage by German agents.

ships might provoke the United States to declare war. They didn't want another powerful nation to enter the conflict on the side of the Allies. However, aware of the Americans' unpreparedness for battle, they decided it was a risk worth taking.

Black Tom Island

The explosion at Black Tom Island on the night of July 30, 1916, is considered by many to be the first foreign terrorist attack on American soil. Tons of gunpowder and TNT, much of which would be shipped to Allied troops, was stored at the munitions depot in New York Harbor. At two o'clock in the morning, an explosion lit up the sky. Fires broke out, and guards called the Jersey City fire department before fleeing for their lives.

The series of blasts that followed caused a force like an earthquake that shook people awake for miles. Many reported being thrown to the floor. Glass shattered throughout Brooklyn and lower Manhattan. Onlookers got down on their knees and prayed as flying shrapnel kept firefighters at bay. Immigrants were evacuated from nearby Ellis Island. Damage to the Statue of Liberty would later cost $100,000 to repair, and ten people died.

US officials could not trace the source of the explosion. They decided that it was accidental. It took years for investigators to realize that a German master spy, Franz von Rintelin, was likely responsible. His weapon of choice was a cigar-sized bomb called a pencil bomb. It was designed using acid that would slowly eat away at the wires inside. It would detonate after a delay of several days. Placed on a ship in port, the bomb would blow up at sea. Von Rintelin may have destroyed up to thirty-six ships and millions of dollars' worth of cargo. He is believed to have bribed a Slovakian immigrant who set the bombs that destroyed the munitions depot at Black Tom Island.

Germ Sabotage

Dr. Anton Dilger was a German-American physician trained at the Johns Hopkins University Medical School. He was on his way to a successful career as a surgeon when Germany entered the war. Dilger had lived in Germany for several years and was sympathetic to the Central Powers' cause. The German Secret Service recruited him as an agent and assigned him a biological warfare task.

Hundreds of thousands of horses and mules were used to move supplies on the battlefield. They

Up to seven thousand horses could be killed in a single World War I battle.

pulled ambulances across muddy terrain and carried messengers and cavalry officers to the front lines. These animals were so important to the war effort that they were even fitted with gas masks to protect from another innovation of World War I, poison gas. Up to seven thousand horses could die in a single battle. Preventing the United States from sending more healthy animals to Europe could undermine the Allies' ability to fight.

Dilger returned to the United States and set up a lab with his brother near Washington, DC. His mission was to infect horses with anthrax and another type of deadly bacteria called glanders. Dock workers accepted bribes to infect horses and mules in several cities. Sometimes these workers accidentally infected themselves. While many animals did sicken and die, the hoped-for outbreak did not occur. One reason was that a recently developed test for glanders was widely used by 1915. Sick animals were identified before they were put on ships, so they did not infect more livestock.

Germans targeted other countries with biological sabotage in addition to America, and the overall impact remains unclear. Eventually falling under suspicion of the US Federal Bureau of Investigation, Dilger fled the United States. Just a few years later, he died in Madrid, Spain, a victim of the Spanish flu pandemic.

The Zimmermann Telegram

In January 1917, the Germans prepared to launch a massive submarine campaign against cargo ships crossing the Atlantic. Shortly thereafter, one of the Room 40 code breakers approached William Hall with shocking information. He had partially unencrypted a message from the German Foreign Secretary, Arthur Zimmermann. Hall believed it might have the potential to change the course of the war.

Further sleuthing revealed that the telegram had been triple-encrypted. Once Room 40 analysts found a way to access all three versions, they were

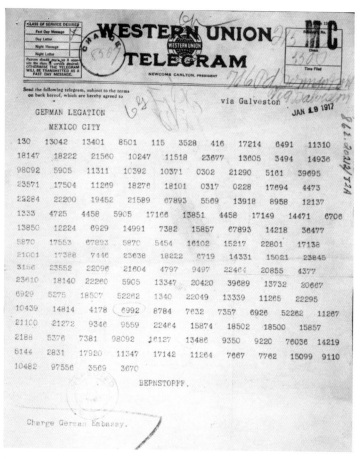

Information in the decrypted Zimmermann Telegram helped motivate the United States to enter World War I.

able to decipher the full message. It revealed that Zimmermann planned to try to form a German alliance with Mexico. Zimmermann also said that Germany would help Mexico invade the United States. In exchange, he wanted the Mexican government to help persuade Japan to join the Central Powers.

Strategic Dilemma

The contents of the Zimmermann telegram were explosive, but Hall was faced with a dilemma. If he revealed the German plan to the Americans, Germany would know the British had intercepted the telegram and cracked the secret codes. They would change their codebooks, and the British would lose a major intelligence advantage. Hall very much wanted America to join the war on the Allies' side. At the same time, he knew he could not compromise the work of Room 40.

At first, Hall decided to do nothing. He destroyed all but one version of the telegram. The remaining one was locked in a safe in his office. He would wait to see what happened. If the Germans started sinking commercial ships, the Americans might enter the conflict on their own, and there would be no need to reveal the contents of the telegram. Hall closely followed the information coming out of Berlin, and on February 1st, open submarine warfare officially began. In response, America ended diplomatic relations with Germany. Wilson said the United States would now follow a policy of "armed neutrality." Hall knew at this point that Wilson remained determined not to declare war unless directly provoked.

Hall finally decided he must tell the Americans what he knew. He also needed to persuade them that the telegram was legitimate without revealing British sources and methods to the world. He conferred with American intelligence officers and diplomats, and it was decided that the Americans would take credit for discovering the information themselves so that Room 40 would not be implicated.

Room 40 employees took the telegram to the American Embassy in London. They brought a copy of the codebook and helped the ambassador decipher

DID YOU KNOW?

Fake trees like this were erected to camouflage soldiers.

At times soldiers had to come up with creative ways to conceal themselves. French soldiers built a papier-mâché dead horse and took turns hiding inside it. In Belgium, Germans cut down a tree at night and replaced it with a hollow replica that would give scouts cover.

the telegram himself. The diplomats could now honestly claim that they had deciphered the telegram on American soil. A copy was immediately sent to President Wilson.

A few days later, US newspapers published the contents of the telegram. Americans were outraged by the Germans' plans. President Wilson and the American public accepted that the time for neutrality was over. On April 6, 1917, largely because of the intelligence uncovered by Room 40, the United States declared war on Germany.

The US Cipher Bureau

The US military struggled to recruit soldiers and to scrape together the trucks, airplanes, and weapons necessary to fight a war. Likewise, intelligence operations also needed to be built from the ground up. Herbert Yardley was a government clerk who loved solving codes and longed to be hired as a cryptologist. When Yardley asked to join the effort, little did he know that the US government did not employ a single dedicated cryptologist. Yardley was put in charge of the whole new eighth section of military intelligence, or MI8.

Professor John Manly was also an amateur code breaker. He had worked as a professor of both mathematics and English literature. When he was fifty-one years old, he volunteered to join the Army. Manly was commissioned as an officer and served in MI8 under Yardley. In 1917, MI8 started with 3 employees and grew to 165 over the year. Manly recruited colleagues such as fellow professor Edith Rickert to join MI8's work.

The Waberski Cipher

In February of 1918, a German spy named Lothar Witzke posed as a Russian national. Traveling under the name Pablo Waberski, he slipped into the United States from Mexico. Federal agents at the border found a coded message sewn into his pocket. This message became known as the Waberski cipher. The agents sent it to Manly for decrypting.

Manly and Rickert worked for seventy-two hours straight to break the complex Waberski cipher. The message identified Witzke as a secret agent. He was ultimately convicted of espionage as a result of their work. The Waberski incident helped establish MI8's importance in supporting the war effort and keeping America safe.

Over the course of the war, MI8 cryptographers analyzed items from postage stamps to musical scores to religious amulets as they looked for secret

Mata Hari

Margarete Gertrud Zelle is better known as Mata Hari. She is considered one of the most famous spies of all time. Of Dutch origin, she moved to Asia with her abusive husband. She eventually divorced and fled to Paris where she reinvented herself, claiming to be a high-class dancer from India named Mata Hari.

Mata Hari was executed for spying.

At the beginning of World War I, she joined the German Secret Service. She traveled through Europe as an entertainer and reported on what she saw to German authorities. Italian intelligence tipped off the French that she was a spy. While they didn't have enough evidence to convict her, the French government started proceedings to have her deported. Mata Hari insisted that she was innocent. To prove it, she offered to spy for the Allies. As she pretended to work for France, she continued to take money from the Germans as a double agent.

Mata Hari's downfall came when she sent a message as ordered by the Germans. However, she used a code that the Germans knew the French had cracked. No longer sure they could trust her, they paid her off and sent her back to Paris. The check from the Germans was all the proof the French needed to arrest her. She was put to death by firing squad on October 15, 1917.

communications. They read more than one hundred thousand messages and decrypted fifty different codes and ciphers from eight foreign governments.

United States Trench Codes

The US military didn't develop its first trench code until 1918. An Army code breaker, Lieutenant J. Rives Childs, was tasked with trying to crack forty-four messages in order to test the code's security. He solved them all in less than a day, negating months of hard work. The entire code had to be scrapped. The US military went back to the drawing board.

This time army cryptographers decided to use a two-part encryption. They also committed to changing the code every two weeks to make it more difficult for enemies to intercept the key. Both these innovations ultimately made their codes more secure than any others in use at the time.

Invisible Ink

Using codes to encrypt messages was one way to keep them secret. Invisible ink was the other. Natural materials had been used for centuries to produce invisible writing. For example, a message produced

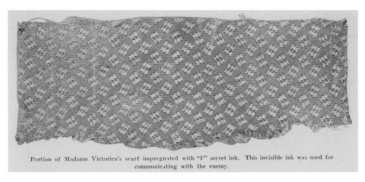

Portion of Madame Victorica's scarf impregnated with "F" secret ink. This invisible ink was used for communicating with the enemy.

German spy Madame Marie de Victorica soaked secret ink into her scarf to conceal and transport it.

by a pen dipped in lemon juice would be unseen. The invisible communication could be written between the lines of a seemingly normal letter until heated, when the lemon juice would turn brown, revealing the secret contents. Another example is sympathetic stains, where the agent used to pen the message was visible only after applying a specific reagent.

The art of invisible ink was still fairly basic at the beginning of the war. After the British intercepted and uncovered several German communications written in secret ink, the Germans realized they needed to explore new techniques and substances that would make the writing more difficult to detect and interpret. German chemists soon developed new and unique types of ink that could be read only after applying the specific chemical reagents. The British and French began to find that although they could tell an intercepted document contained secret writing, they had no idea how to reveal it. The Allies in turn set up several secret ink laboratories where they experimented with chemicals that would let them decipher the Germans' new ink formulations.

German spies on the move had to devise clever ways to carry inks and reagents in order to conceal them from the enemy in case of capture. Often, everyday items like mouthwash or shampoo bottles with false labels were used. Sometimes the ink was soaked into clothing items such as scarves or handkerchiefs. They had to be careful not to expose these items to heat or sunlight, which might cause the ink to change color and be discovered.

The Maud Letter

In early 1917, a German spy named Madame Marie de Victorica moved to New York City. She joined a German espionage ring already operating in the city. Her mission was to help smuggle explosives into the country. She planned to conceal the materials inside hollow religious statues of the saints. The explosives would eventually be used to plant bombs on American ships.

On one of Victorica's first walks around her new neighborhood, she stopped at the shop of a German

La Dame Blanche

A British agent named Harry Landau devised a unique way to collect information about German trains passing through Belgium. He recruited a group of everyday citizens, whose spy network became known as La Dame Blanche (French for "the White Lady"). They were named after an old legend that the German Kaiser would be defeated when the White Lady appeared.

Belgian merchants used innovative means such as hollowed-out brooms to get information across the Dutch border to Landau. For example, beans indicated the number of German soldiers, guns, and horses on trains steaming toward the front lines of battle. These merchant spies also concealed messages in common goods such as chocolates and soaps. When they were busy keeping shop, their children took over the important work of counting the trains.

Belgian train engineers also contributed to the resistance effort. They opened and closed their fireboxes in a series of short and long intervals that mimicked the dots and dashes of Morse Code. These signals conveyed information about German troop movements to the British.

chemist for a prearranged meeting. He supplied her with the reagents she needed to develop the secret messages she would receive. The letters, which seemed to convey mundane information, soon followed. In reality, they were written in a combination of code and invisible ink. Reading them was a laborious process. Not only did Victorica have to apply and develop the reagent, but then she had to unencrypt the coded text.

After the United States entered the war, Victorica's mission became more dangerous. Several of her fellow spies were arrested. She suspected that she was being followed and moved to a different hotel. Couriers sent to bring her money or ink reagents were sometimes arrested before they reached her. Without the proper chemicals, she couldn't read important messages sent from Germany. Without enough money, she grew increasingly desperate. A mix-up at the post office compounded her troubles.

Mass Surveillance

During World War I, the US Postal Service began monitoring all mail originating from Europe with the aim of intercepting war-related intelligence. Many letters therefore failed to reach their destinations. To increase the odds of successful receipt, Germans often sent multiple copies of secret messages. The letters might bear different signatures to make them look like separate pieces of correspondence. They might go to different addresses altogether.

In January of 1918, a courier mixed up two similar letters. As a result, the one intended for Victorica was sent to the wrong address and intercepted by a censor. Because it bore a signature that read "Maud," it became known as the Maud letter. The Maud letter wound up in the hands of Dr. Emmett Carver, the head of New York's military secret ink lab. He was able to reveal the secret writing and even took a quick photograph before it disappeared. Now the government had hard evidence against one of the city's most prominent spies.

Meanwhile, hoping for financial help from agents in Mexico, Victorica wrote messages on six tiny slips of paper. She hired someone to roll them into cigars and then deliver them. On April 16, 1918, her plea was answered. Victorica's maid left a folded newspaper on

DID YOU KNOW?

In England, no spies were captured or executed after 1916. The government concluded that either the Germans had given up or they had gotten so much better at espionage that they avoided detection.

a pew in St. Patrick's Cathedral. A man with his own newspaper then sat down in the pew. The money was tucked inside the paper, and he made a surreptitious exchange. Federal agents watched the whole process from afar. They arrested Victorica less than two weeks later. She was convicted of spying and died in prison in 1920. Other arrests followed. The spy ring dissolved, its mission unfulfilled. Victorica and the other agents had spent so much time planning that they never got around to importing explosives or causing any damage.

Everyday Spies

The war was long, and as each scheme for delivering information was discovered, new and creative ways to keep communications secret were implemented. A massive number of means and civilians were involved in spying. Subterfuge seemed everywhere. Even the spinning of windmills was more than it appeared— Germans spun the sails to relay messages in a method that simulated Morse Code.

Food and consumer goods became vehicles for communication. The items displayed in a bakery window in Russia relayed secret German reports. Local inspectors stamped day—old bread with a number to indicate it was no longer fresh. The Polish arranged the numbers stamped on the loaves to help spies arrange meetings with government officials. Each spy was assigned a number. If he saw his number in the window, he knew he had an assignment. A Peruvian-born German ran a shipping business as a front for his espionage activities. He hid information about British Naval operations in the invoices for his canned sardines. He was caught when British agents realized that sardines were out of season in winter. He was executed by firing squad at the Tower of London.

Two other German spies posed as cigar merchants. The number and brands of cigars in their shipments stood for information about British ships' locations. They didn't realize that British sailors smoked cigarettes or pipes rather than cigars. They met the same fate as the spy who shipped sardines.

Historians estimate that thousands of spies died in World War I. German agent Carl Lody was the first person executed at the Tower of London in over 150 years. Eleven enemy agents were shot at the Tower of London over the course of the war, and one was hanged. Most of them were caught because of intercepted intelligence. They were executed in public in hopes of deterring other spies.

IMPACT AND LEGACY

Technological advances made during World War I forever changed the way battles would be fought. Electric lanterns allowed troops and ships to move more freely at night. Battleships, tanks, and fighter planes were used for the first time. The swift adoption of these new technologies was mirrored in public life. Cars and airplanes had been relatively rare before the war. After its conclusion, they would be everywhere.

Espionage methods quickly adapted to the new technologies. Cryptanalysts also made huge advances in code breaking over the course of World War I.

OPPOSITE:
The Enigma machine revolutionized cryptogrphy.

As they developed increasingly sophisticated ciphers, they also learned to solve them. Their achievements created a cycle that propelled more and more innovation.

ADGFVX

The Germans invented a complex cipher called ADGFVX in March 1918. In April, French cryptanalyst Lieutenant Georges Painvin cracked the code and learned the location the Germans intended to attack. The French placed their troops strategically and won the battle.

The Germans unveiled a new and improved ADGFVX cipher in June. They believed that this version was unbreakable. Painvin worked so long and hard on unencrypting it that he lost thirty pounds in the process. Within weeks, he had deciphered it. Almost every cipher system created during the conflict was broken by the time the war ended. Cryptanalysts' advancing skills meant that new methods must be developed to make communication secure.

Code Talkers

The Allies knew the enemy was eavesdropping on radio communications, but they believed telephone conversations were secure. In the middle of the war, the Germans invented a machine called the Moritz. It allowed them to tap phone lines and listen in on the Allies' phone calls. The Moritz was not easy to use. German soldiers crawled along the ground to bury copper plates that would serve as conductors. These amplified the current from the telephone wires and let Germans hear what was being said. Eventually, the Allies realized what the Germans were up to. Without secure telephones, the Allies needed to either speak in code or send false messages to trick the eavesdroppers.

In the fall of 1918, the Germans had tapped into phone lines on the western front of battle. The Central Powers had successfully unscrambled American codes and were capturing their foot messengers. American commanders were at a loss for how to communicate securely with their troops until a captain happened to overhear a conversation between two soldiers in their native Choctaw language.

Choctaw was a language spoken by relatively few people and unfamiliar to most if not all Europeans. Its grammar and syntax were completely different from Romance and Germanic languages. There was no written Choctaw dictionary that the enemy could use to try to learn the lexicon. All these conditions made it perfect for conveying secret information.

Fortunately, there was another Choctaw-speaking soldier at headquarters who could receive messages translated by the soldiers on the front lines. The Germans had no idea what to make of the unfamiliar language they subsequently heard over the airwaves. It was impossible for them to decode. The Allies soon gained the upper hand in the battle.

The Choctaw language became a powerful weapon against the enemy—ironically, given that the US government was trying to eliminate the tribe's native tongue back at home. Choctaw children were punished for speaking their language at school. Nonetheless, it survived. Nineteen Choctaw soldiers were recruited

Members of the Choctaw Telephone Squad helped the Allies convey secret intelligence.

to join the telephone squad. While the Choctaw language did not include words for many modern military concepts, the men made up their own terms to convey what they needed to say. Had the war gone on longer, there would likely have been more soldiers added to this detail. However, this was the last major campaign on the Western Front before World War I ended on November 11, 1918. Twenty years later, the intelligence community remembered the usefulness of Native Americans, and hundreds of Navajo Code Talkers were called to service and trained for battle during World War II.

Enter the Machines

World War I would be the last war that involved cryptologists hunched over desks with paper and pencils, engaged in the battle of the wits against mindboggling puzzles. As the volume of intercepted messages increased, cryptanalysis involved larger numbers of personnel crunching huge amounts of data. It became less of a linguistic feat than a mathematical and statistical one. Machines came into use for both encryption and decryption, making codebooks obsolete. The first of these machines were developed during World War I.

Random Problem

In 1918, cryptographers experimented with cipher keys that were completely random. US Major Joseph Mauborgne introduced the concept of a random key that would be used only one time. Making it secure would require a very long key. It would be written on two pads of paper, one for the sender and one for the recipient. Each would be several hundred pages long. After its use, the "one-time pad key" as it came to be called would be destroyed. A new random key would then be developed.

The cipher described by Mauborgne would truly be unbreakable, as cryptanalysts' work was all about analyzing patterns. Random codes have no patterns. Because of the length of the key, analysts would have to try five hundred octillion combinations of letters to deduce the solution. Even if it were humanly possible to do the calculation, there would still be

Cipher disks have been used for centuries to generate random substitutions.

multiple possible keys. Due to the random nature of the substitutions, there would be no way to distinguish the right translation from the wrong ones.

While the one-time pad cipher was a theoretically sound idea, it could not be practically implemented. Given the number of messages that needed to be exchanged, there was no realistic way to generate enough unique random keys. Operators tried making keys by randomly pecking away at typewriters but soon discovered that they typed letters in predictable sequences. Distributing a large number of unique keys also presented its own challenges.

A truly practical random key, analysts realized, would have to be mechanically generated. This idea was not new. An invention from the fifteenth century called the cipher disk was a basic mechanical method of scrambling characters to encrypt messages. Cryptographers, having now exhausted every human-generated option they could think of, realized that a more sophisticated version of the cipher disk could help make ciphers much more secure.

Enigma

In 1915, the Dutch developed a cipher-making machine prototype. It was powered by a rotor and was based on the operational principles of a cipher disk. This machine was a precursor to a model developed by German inventor Arthur Scherbius in 1918. His first device, the Enigma A, used a typewriter-like keyboard and an electrically powered internal wheel to automatically generate and print codes. The Enigma A was large, expensive, and not terribly reliable.

Scherbius continued honing its design. Later versions displayed output using glow lamps rather than printing it on paper. The Enigma machine sent plaintext through three different wheels, then

Drones

At the outset of World War I, the United States military possessed fewer than three hundred aircraft. Most generals did not initially see how airplanes could be useful in battle. The main function of planes at the beginning of the war was aerial surveillance. As the conflict wore on, the military began to develop bomber and fighter planes. The first ace fighter pilots fought in World War I, quickly changing the nature of the war.

Kettering's Bug was a precursor to the first true drones.

In the United States, Orville Wright and engineer Charles Kettering spearheaded a secret project in 1918. They wondered whether it would be possible to design a pilot-less plane. They developed an aircraft known as "the self-flying aerial torpedo," or "Kettering's Bug." They ultimately built fifty of the flying machines, but the war ended before they could be deployed in battle. The reliability of these unmanned planes was never really tested, but they are considered precursors of the first true drones of the 1950s.

used a reflector to send it back through the machine, essentially scrambling it six times over.

The usefulness of this machine was clear to intelligence analysts, but its expense deterred investors, especially since the war was over. Then in 1924, Winston Churchill published a book that described how Germany's secret codebooks had been stolen during the war and used by Room 40 to gain a huge intelligence advantage. The Germans were shocked, ten years later, to learn how their secret communications had been compromised. Seeking a solution, they hit upon the Enigma machine.

Over the next twenty years, Germany bought more than thirty thousand Enigma machines. By the time World War II erupted, the Germans had the most secure cryptographic system on the planet.

Patriotism

The spy fever Britain experienced before World War I transformed to panic and paranoia among the public and around the world. Suspicion ran wild, and many innocent people were unjustly accused of working as spies. A French shepherd was accused of rounding up his sheep in patterns so he could pass messages to the Germans. British soldiers sliced open dead fish in a futile hunt for messages planted inside by the Germans. They interrogated farmers suspected of hiding messages in the furrows of their fields.

In the United States, an ultra-patriotic environment prevailed. Numerous groups sprang up with names such as Knights of Liberty, Sedition Slammers, and Terrible Threateners. Their goal was to ensure that all Americans fully participated in the war effort. They intended to root out any hint of dissent or disloyalty.

The best-known of these groups was the American Protective League (APL), which had 250,000 civilian members in six hundred cities. President Wilson approved the organization's formation, and the Department of Justice supported and endorsed their activities. Many members even wore official-looking badges that read "Secret Service." They targeted immigrants, socialists, anti-war protesters, and anyone suspected of sympathizing with the enemy. They raided businesses, routinely surveilled private citizens, and worked with local police departments to round up any citizens they suspected of disloyalty.

The APL was disbanded three months after the war ended. However, echoes of their activities are still felt today in a highly partisan environment, where dissent is often considered unpatriotic and threats against Muslims have proliferated since the terrorist attacks on September 11, 2001.

The United States Espionage Act

Enemy spies living in the United States were a real danger, as evidenced by incidents such as the Black Tom Island explosion. Investigators found clear evidence of German plots to take over American newspapers to spread propaganda and even to blow up important transportation corridors. The legitimate fear of German spies led many Americans to be suspicious of all German immigrants. Anti-German sentiment reached a fevered pitch during the war. German words were even purged from restaurant menus. Sauerkraut was temporarily known as liberty cabbage.

In this environment of mass paranoia, Congress passed the United States Espionage Act in 1917. The law was not intended to stifle political dissent. Instead, it was conceived as a way to counter real threats from traitorous individuals. Its scope was hotly debated by Congress. Some legislators wanted to place restrictions on freedom of the press, but this proposal was rejected as a violation of First Amendment rights.

Despite legislators' care to ensure the law was not interpreted too broadly, its language resulted in a nationwide crackdown on anyone seen as unsupportive of the war effort. The Postmaster General effectively censored anti-war publications by refusing to let them use the mail service. Prosecutors filed ill-conceived charges against peaceful protestors and law-abiding German Americans. One filmmaker was put on trial for making a movie about the American Revolution that showed the British in a bad light, because it was seen as derogatory towards the Allies. Socialist Eugene Debs was jailed for making a public statement about the importance of freedom. Fifteen hundred arrests were made under the US Espionage Act and the even more restrictive amendments known as the Sedition Act. Only ten of these arrests involved actual war crimes or sabotage.

While the Sedition Act was repealed at the end of the war, the Espionage Act remains in effect. It is used to this day to prosecute those who are accused of threatening national security, and its application remains controversial. Today's surveillance of civilians by the US government also has its roots in the domestic spying on German Americans and others during World War I.

Radio for the Masses

At the beginning of the war, troops used horse-drawn wagons to laboriously lay miles of telegraph cable along the front lines. But the telegram quickly proved itself an impractical way to communicate when the speedier and more mobile radio was invented.

At first, radio had its drawbacks. The technology was cumbersome and difficult to transport into battle, due to the heavy vacuum tubes. In addition, horses had to be fitted with hand-cranked generators strapped to their saddles to power the units.

When the US government took over the private airwaves in 1917, huge investments were made in radio technology. Over the course of the war, transmitters and units became increasingly smaller. Airplanes and ships began to employ radios. Signal strength and broadcasting range increased. By 1918, the units used by soldiers bore little resemblance to those at the beginning of the war.

Soon after World War I, the first commercial radio stations were established. The radio entertainment industry was born. Music stations, news, and serialized dramas would soon populate the airwaves. The president could use radio to communicate directly with the American people. Propaganda was also easier to disseminate as broadcasts reached hundreds of thousands of citizens in real time.

World War I field radios were large and not as widely used on land as they would be once the technology became smaller.

The Black Chamber

Despite its late start, the US Army intelligence service managed to effectively catch up to the rest of the world by the end of the war. Post-war budget cuts then forced the government to disband it. A civilian agency was established in its place. This was the first national intelligence agency in US history. Herbert Yardley, former head of MI8, was chosen to lead the agency, which was known as the Cipher Bureau. It was headquartered in New York City.

The Cipher Bureau was so secret that when President Hoover was elected in 1928, his Secretary of State, Henry Stimson, didn't know it existed. When Stimson found out, he was furious. He saw no purpose to their work during peace time. He also didn't believe that it was mannerly or ethical to read other people's mail.

The US government dissolved the Cipher Bureau in 1929 and transferred signal intelligence operations back to the military Signal Corps. A controversial figure, Yardley was offered a position at the Army's new cryptologic organization, but at a much lower salary. He declined. Now unemployed and with a family to support during the Great Depression, Yardley needed a source of income. He decided to write about his experiences as a covert operative.

Yardley's story appeared as a magazine serial before it was collected in a best-selling book, *The American Black Chamber*, in 1932. Many working cryptanalysts were horrified by the secrets he revealed. They claimed the book undermined national security. Yardley countered that the reason he'd written the book was to expose flaws in US intelligence operations that needed to be addressed. Congress soon passed a law that would prevent the publication of tell-all books revealing government secrets.

National Security Agencies

At the beginning of World War I, there were only three United States soldiers trained in code breaking.

The Army assigned none of them jobs in cryptology. The history of US intelligence up until the war involved many scattered efforts. There had been no sustained, systematic attempt to regularly collect intelligence.

In 1865, the US Signal Corps became the first intelligence operation that wasn't disbanded after a conflict ended. Various departmental reorganizations resulted in no agency with enough power or budget to produce useful intelligence by 1908. This situation finally changed in May of 1917 with the creation of the Military Intelligence Section. Its name was later changed to the Military Intelligence Division, and one legacy of World War I was the post-war formation of the Cipher Bureau.

The National Security Agency (NSA) is headquartered in Fort Meade, Maryland.

The Black Chamber, otherwise known as the Cipher Bureau, was a precursor to US government agencies dedicated to intelligence gathering. Today, the Central Intelligence Agency (CIA), established in 1947, is responsible for training and deploying international spies. Cryptography and signals intelligence is the domain of the National Security Agency (NSA), founded in 1952.

In Great Britain, the Government Code and Ciphers Training School was established in 1919 and employed many signals intelligence specialists who had worked in Room 40. These men and women paved the way for the analysts at Bletchley Park who would play a key role in World War II. The more well-known successes of the Bletchley Park code breakers would never have been possible without the advances made by cryptographers of Room 40.

In its day, World War I was called the Great War or the War to End All Wars. People believed that the horrors of the conflict would inspire humans to choose peace in the future. But twenty years later, the world would be at war again. The lessons of World War I would have a huge influence on the outcome of World War II and beyond.

Chronology

1909 The British government founds the Secret Service Bureau.

1914 Archduke Ferdinand is assassinated, sparking World War I. The British begin recruiting cryptographers to work in Room 40. Intercepted intelligence helps the Germans crush the Russians in the Battle of Tannenberg.

1916 The Black Tom Island munitions depot explodes in New York.

1917 British cryptanalysts decipher the Zimmermann Telegram. The United States declares war on Germany. The US Military Intelligence Section is established. US Congress passes the Espionage Act.

1918 The United States military develops its first trench code. The Germans invent the ADGFVX cipher. Enigma A is invented. World War I ends.

1919 The British government founds the Government Code and Ciphers Training School.

1929 The US government dissolves the Cipher Bureau.

1947 The US government establishes the Central Intelligence Agency (CIA).

1952 The US government establishes the National Security Agency (NSA).

Glossary

cryptanalyst A person who analyzes and deciphers secret codes.

cryptographer A person who creates and writes secret codes.

cryptologist A person who studies both cryptanalysis and cryptography.

decryption Decoding of an encrypted message.

deported Forced to leave the country.

double agent A spy who is working for one entity while pretending to work for another.

encryption The process of encoding messages.

espionage The practice of being a spy.

infiltrate To get access to an organization or group through deceit.

linguist A person who studies languages.

plaintext The original text of a message before it is translated to code.

reagent A chemical agent that produces a reaction.

reconnaissance Observation of an area to obtain information about its layout and feature

subterfuge Trickery or deceit.

surveillance Observation.

Books

Atwood, Kathryn J. *Women Heroes of World War I: 16 Remarkable Resisters, Soldiers, Spies, and Medics.* Chicago, IL: Chicago Review Press, Incorporated, 2016.

Goodman, Michael E. *World War I Spies.* Mankato, MN: Creative Education and Creative Paperbacks, 2016.

Janeczko, Paul. *Top Secret: A Handbook of Codes, Ciphers, and Secret Writing.* Boston, MA: Candlewick, 2006.

Websites

CIA Kids' Zone

https://www.cia.gov/kids-page

The CIA provides activities and information for middle and high school students related to code breaking and espionage.

International Spy Museum

https://www.spymuseum.org/

The International Spy Museum's website gives information about visiting the Washington, DC museum, includes interactive exhibits, and suggests activities for families.

Selected Bibliography

Cellan-Jones, Rory. "Pigeon vs Telephone: Which Worked Best in the Trenches?" BBC IWonder. Accessed October 02, 2017. http://www.bbc.co.uk/guides/zw6gq6f.

Cockroft, Steph. "The First Bletchley Park: New Exhibition Reveals the Secrets of Room 40 Where Codebreakers Became the Hidden Heroes Who Won World War One." Daily Mail Online. July 30, 2015. Accessed October 04, 2017. http://www.dailymail.co.uk/news/article-3179749/The-Bletchley-Park-New-exhibition-reveals-secrets-Room-40-codebreakers-hidden-heroes-won-World-War-One.html.

Dooley, John. *Codes, Ciphers and Spies: Tales of Military Intelligence in World War I*. Springer, 2016. Electronic.

Downing, Taylor. *Secret Warriors: The Spies, Scientists and Code Breakers of World War I*. New York: Pegasus Books, 2014.

Dubenskij, Charlotte. "World War One: How Radio Crackled into Life in Conflict." BBC News. June 18, 2014. Accessed October 04, 2017. http://www.bbc.com/news/uk-wales-27894944.

Hughes-Wilson, John. *Secret State: A History of Intelligence and Espionage*. New York: Pegasus Books, 2016.

Inman, Michael. "Spies Among Us: World War I and The American Protective League." The New York Public Library. February 02, 2015. Accessed October 04, 2017. https://www.nypl.org/blog/2014/10/07/spies-among-us-wwi-apl.

King, Gilbert. "Sabotage in New York Harbor." Smithsonian.com. November 01, 2011. Accessed

October 03, 2017. https://www.smithsonianmag.
com/history/sabotage-in-new-york-
harbor-123968672/.

King, Melanie. "Thanks for the Spycraft, World War I -
The Boston Globe." BostonGlobe.com. August 03,
2014. Accessed September 30, 2017. https://www.
bostonglobe.com/ideas/2014/08/02/thanks-for-
spycraft-world-war/lrjmteHDfRevXdP9qGACHN/
story.html.

Myre, Greg. "From Wristwatches To Radio, How World
War I Ushered In The Modern World." NPR. April
02, 2017. Accessed October 04, 2017. http://www.
npr.org/sections/parallels/2017/04/02/521792062/
from-wristwatches-to-radio-how-world-war-i-
ushered-in-the-modern-world.

NSA. "Pearl Harbor Review." The Black Chamber.
May 03, 2016. Accessed October 04, 2017. https://
www.nsa.gov/about/cryptologic-heritage/center-
cryptologic-history/pearl-harbor-review/black-

Richelson, Jeffrey T. *A Century of Spies: Intelligence
in the Twentieth Century*. New York: Oxford Univ.
Press, 1997.

Singh, Simon. *The Code Book*. New York, NY: Delacorte
Press, 2003.

Tagg, Lori. "Army's First Cipher Office Broke the Code
on Modern Cryptology." Www.army.mil. July 7,
2017. Accessed October 03, 2017. https://www.
army.mil/article/190449/armys_first_cipher_
office_broke_the_code_on_modern_cryptology.

Winterman, Denise. "World War One: The Original
Code Talkers." BBC News. May 19, 2014. Accessed
October 03, 2017. http://www.bbc.com/news/
magazine-26963624.

Index

Jeanne Marie Ford is an Emmy-winning television scriptwriter and holds an MFA in Writing for Children from Vermont College. A cryptologist's daughter, she has written numerous books on a variety of subjects, including World War I. She also teaches college English. She lives in Maryland with her husband and two children.